THE SUPER SHOPPER

SUPERMARKET SECRETS

By Robyn Freedman Spizman
Published by Ivy Books:

GETTING ORGANIZED
KITCHEN 101
FREE AND FABULOUS
SUPERMARKET SECRETS
MEALS IN MINUTES*
QUICK TIPS FOR BUSY PEOPLE*

*Forthcoming

THE SUPER SHOPPER

SUPERMARKET SECRETS

Robyn Freedman Spizman

IVY BOOKS • NEW YORK

An Ivy Book
Published by The Ballantine Publishing Group
Copyright © 1998 by Robyn Freedman Spizman

Cover photo © Philip Shone Photography

http://www.randomhouse.com

Library of Congress Catalog Card Number: 97-94253

ISBN 0-8041-1681-4

Manufactured in the United States of America

First Edition: May 1998

10 9 8 7 6 5 4 3 2 1

This book is dedicated to you, the reader, for caring enough, worrying enough, and being conscientious enough to want to provide yourself and your family with the best! And to my wonderful parents, Phyllis and Jack Freedman; my husband, Willy; and our children, Justin and Ali, for endless servings of love and support.

Contents

Acknowledgments

It's no secret that books couldn't be published without an endless group of dedicated people working hard to make them happen. And this project was no exception. My unending thanks go to my literary agent, Meredith Bernstein; my editor, Elisa Wares; Laura Paczosa; and everyone at The Ballantine Publishing Group who contributed the necessary ingredients to make this book possible. A very special thank-you to the talented Mary Ann Lukas of Harry's Farmers Market for her insights and assistance with the information presented in this book. Her commitment to helping me uncover the slew of super secrets we discovered will always be appreciated. Many thanks also go to Bettye Storne for her valuable help in and out of the kitchen.

Introduction:
Calling All Shoppers!

As a television consumer advocate for over fifteen years, I have been called the Super Shopper. I earned this title because I have discovered super tips that really help make life easier. In this day and age, everyone needs to be a super shopper, and the goal of this book is to help you make smart decisions as you shop and prepare meals for yourself and your family.

When it comes to shopping, some of the best trade secrets I have learned over the years have been discovered at—you guessed it—the supermarket! From the produce aisle to the seafood counter, there is a wealth of information locked inside those containers and packages displayed on the shelves. I can reassure you that all produce and products aren't created equally. As I collected the tips included in this book, the wealth of information and food facts we need to be super shoppers amazed me.

So shoppers, take your mark! With this book in hand, you'll have simple tips that will not only make you a smart shopper, but also put the food you purchase to use more wisely once you bring it home. *Supermarket Secrets* is jam-packed with smart advice and helpful tips that have worked for other shoppers. You'll learn how to make each product count.

I hope that these secrets will help you purchase products and prepare food more wisely. By following the tips in this book, you'll save money and time and make better choices.

Speaking of shopping, think for a moment: what type of shopper are you? Do you speedshop, racing down each aisle? Do you grab and go? Or do you pore over every label carefully and check the ingredients in each item? Do you read the cans, inspect the fruit, and look at dates? When preparing food, are you certain it's fresh and safely stored? In many cases we forget to check things or don't always know what to do. The old rule "When in doubt, throw it out" takes over. Regardless of what kind of shopper you are, fast and furious or slow and diligent, equipped with the information in this book you will have the know-how right now to shop smart.

This book has a wealth of information that will help you in a variety of areas at the grocery store and then at home in your kitchen. The tips are separated into categories, and each chapter will assist you in unlocking the simple secrets that every shopper needs to know: Learn more about what you are buying and ultimately eating. Question your grocery choices. And stop yourself from making costly mistakes. From avoiding food spoilage to food safety measures, *Super-*

market Secrets will give you aisles of information
to help you make the most of your grocery shopping and food preparation experiences.

Note: Every effort was made to insure that the safety and
nutritional information in this book were as up-to-date
as possible at the time of publication.

1

Secrets About the Produce Department

What could be more dazzling than the color, texture, freshness, and variety of the produce department? Thanks to modern transport technology, refrigeration, and storage facilities, an overwhelming variety of fresh produce enters our grocery stores and farmers' markets daily. We are no longer limited to specific growing seasons. But how do you know what's in season? What's the best way to select a certain vegetable or fruit? How do you prevent spoilage? How do you prepare fruits and vegetables to maximize their flavor and taste?

The following tips will help you make better choices when selecting produce. They will also assist you in extending the life of your fruits and vegetables and make them last longer.

Selecting Fruit

• When selecting fruit or produce, be sure to look for freshness. Avoid any produce that is rotting or has soft spots, blemishes, or punctures.

Fruits such as apricots, all types of melons, and pineapples should have a sweet, fresh scent.

- If you are a regular shopper at one particular store, try to get to know the produce manager. He or she can help in your selection and also keep you up-to-date on seasonal produce.

- Choose citrus fruit (oranges, grapefruit, tangerines, lemons, etc.) mostly by weight. The heaviest fruit will contain the most juice. Look for firm, taut, brightly colored skins.

- Apples should be firm with an even background color and no visible bruises. When stored in the refrigerator, they can last up to a month.

- Bananas should be smooth and have a soft, plump skin with no bruises or dark spots. Dark bananas are a sign of aging.

- Apricots should give slightly when gently pressed. Choose fragrant apricots with a red blush. Avoid apricots that are hard and greenish yellow or soft and mushy. Use ripe apricots immediately or refrigerate up to two days in a plastic bag. To ripen, place in a closed paper bag in a warm room. To peel, drop into boiling water for ten seconds. Remove with a slotted spoon into an ice-water bath. Skin will slip off easily.

- Pears should be fragrant and free of blemishes. Keep pears at room temperature until they ripen slightly; then store them in the refrigerator. The color of ripe pears depends on their variety, but to determine the ripeness of any pear variety, gently press the pear at stem end. A ripe pear will give to gentle pressure.

- Plums should be firm but not hard, yielding slightly to pressure. Avoid plums with a brownish discoloration.
- Grapes should be firm and plump with no signs of withering. They should have a good aroma. Before refrigerating grapes, remove all spoiled ones. Store under refrigeration in a plastic bag.
- Strawberries should be uniform in color and fragrant. Check for fresh-looking hulls, and avoid strawberries with white shoulders. Refrigerate berries unwashed in a plastic bag. They are best when used within 1 to 2 days.
- Melons such as honeydew, cantaloupe, crenshaw, and casaba should feel heavy for their size and should have a sweet aroma. They should also give slightly to pressure. Avoid melons that are soft or that have spots or cracks.
- Pineapples should feel heavy and have a sweet aroma. Leaves should pull easily away from the stem. The fruit should yield slightly to gentle pressure. Make sure that the bottom is not soft or rotted. Once you have the pineapple home, remove the stem to allow for easier storage in the refrigerator.
- Kiwifruit should be plump and unwrinkled and show no visible signs of damage to the exterior. A kiwifruit is ripe and ready to prepare when it yields to gentle pressure.

More Tips About Fruit

- To extract the most juice from fresh lemons, limes, and oranges, roll them between the palm of your hand and the kitchen counter. Lemons also yield more juice when slightly warm or at room temperature.

- When grating lemon for zest, be sure to grate only the peel; the white part is unpleasantly bitter. Try placing a piece of parchment paper over the grater, and it will separate the zest, keeping the bitter pith separate.
- When properly refrigerated, lemons and limes should last up to a month.
- Peeled or cut fruits that oxidize rapidly (bananas, apples, pears, etc.) should be sprinkled with citrus juice to slow their browning.
- Use fresh grapefruit juice to baste chicken or fish as it's baking for added taste.
- Use fresh-squeezed grapefruit juice in place of salt if you are on a low-sodium diet.
- To make a quick and easy dessert, why not make fruit kabobs? Use any combination of fresh fruit pieces and cubes, such as strawberries, kiwi, mango, watermelon, star fruit, grapes, or melons. Place on bamboo skewers and enjoy!
- Add fresh orange juice to pancake batter for a tasty flavor enhancer.
- Apples will not crack while they are baking if you peel a one-inch band around the middle or top.
- Add apple cider to your favorite stuffing, instead of the usual broth, for a delicious change. This is especially good when served with turkey or chicken.
- An easy way to peel peaches is to dip them in boiling water for one minute.

- Freeze berries in a single layer on a baking sheet. When they are frozen, transfer them into freezer containers. Frozen blueberries can be stored for up to two years. The berries will be somewhat softer, but will still retain their flavor. Once they are frozen, be sure and use them for baking.
- To make fruits sparkle, brush the fruits with beaten egg white, then roll them in sugar. They will look as if they have been dusted with snow. This trick makes a great garnish for desserts or surrounding your holiday platter. Suitable fruits include grapes, lady apples, and berries. But don't eat fruit thus treated.
- Strawberries are a highly perishable fruit. Carefully wash them just before using.
- A fast way to hull strawberries is to use a plastic drinking straw. Simply insert straw into the top half of the strawberry; push directly through and out the end. Be sure to remove any leaves before inserting the straw.
- Awaken your taste buds with fresh strawberry pancakes for breakfast. Fill layers of hot pancakes with butter or margarine and fresh strawberry slices. Top with more slices and dust with powdered sugar.
- Fresh strawberries add bright color, sweet taste, and texture to fresh fruit salads and compotes.
- Toss fresh strawberries with aged balsamic vinegar and a pinch of sugar for a fabulous salad substitute. Or add strawberries to your next salad recipe for a festive touch.

- Make a delicious strawberry cooler by combining equal amounts of sliced strawberries, yogurt, and milk. Sweeten with honey to taste. This also works well with overripe bananas and fruit that has become a little too soft.
- When freezing berries, a good way to avoid freezer burn is to place the berries in a zip-type bag. Close the bag almost all the way and insert a plastic drinking straw in the small opening. Suck the air from the bag and close it. This creates a vacuum seal that not only better preserves the fruit but flattens the bag, allowing more room in your freezer.

Selecting Vegetables

- Buyer beware! Make sure the vegetables you choose are fresh and free of blemishes, bruises, and mold. If it's limp or looks like it is wilting, leave it. Inquire whether there is any fresher produce and don't be shy about asking. You deserve the best!
- Often the top layer of produce is picked over, so don't be afraid to check the next layer. It could be fresher and more appealing, or older and not as nice.
- Select tomatoes that are fragrant and have good color. They should be slightly firm yet not too soft. The skin should be smooth and without blemishes.
- Choose broccoli that is tight with a fresh green color and without any yellowed or

brown florets. They should be firm without wilted leaves.

- Select carrots that are firm, not rubbery. They should be brightly colored, not pale. After beets, carrots have the highest sugar content of any vegetable.

- Choose celery that has firm, not rubbery or limp, stalks, with a fresh light green color. The deeper the green, the stronger the flavor.

- Look for corn that has fresh green husks and silk that is not dried out. Kernels should be full and not withered looking. Corn should be cooked as soon as possible after buying to ensure freshness. It loses its natural sugar content rapidly.

- Sweet peppers or bell peppers should be firm and shiny without any signs of bruising or soft or shriveled spots. The heavier the peppers are, the thicker the walls will be inside.

- Potatoes should be firm and smooth. Avoid potatoes with wrinkled or wilted skins or ones that have soft, dark spots, cut surfaces, or a green appearance. For even cooking, choose potatoes that are uniform in size.

- Artichokes should be heavy for their size, compact, and firm, with a soft green color. During the winter, some artichokes might appear slightly bronzed due to exposure to light frost. Bronzing does not affect flavor or texture. Avoid artichokes that are wilted, dry, or moldy. Do not wash them before refrigerating. To store them longer than a few days, drizzle a few drops of water on each one and place in a plastic bag, seal airtight, and refrigerate. Wash artichokes just before preparing.

- Select cauliflower that does not have any dark spots or mold on it.
- Choose beans that are firm with smooth pods, preferably with good color and no discoloration.
- While mushrooms come in all shapes and sizes, their size does not indicate quality. Mushrooms should have a fresh, well-shaped appearance and a firm texture, and be free of spots. The freshest mushrooms are closed around the stem. Refrigerate mushrooms immediately after buying them and store them in a paper-towel-covered container up to 3 days. You must take them out of the plastic bag or they will darken and become very soft.
- When selecting an eggplant, be aware that male eggplants are sweeter and have fewer seeds. To determine an eggplant's gender, look at the bottom of it where the flower was once attached. The male eggplant will have a well-rounded bottom with a smooth, even stem area. The female has a narrow bottom with an indented stem area.
- To ripen fresh tomatoes fast, simply place them in a brown paper bag. Tomatoes naturally release ethylene gas, which makes them ripen faster. Avoid storing tomatoes in the refrigerator. They will become too mushy and lose their flavor.
- Summer squash should be firm with shiny, tender rinds. Color should be consistent with the variety. Avoid squash that show signs of

injury or have pitted or dull skin. In many cases, the smaller the summer squash, the more tender and flavorful it will be.

- Green tomatoes are really red tomatoes that were picked very early, before they became ripe.
- Avoid zucchini with large yellow spots on the skin.

More Tips About Vegetables

- When cooking vegetables in water, be sure to leave them whole. They will retain more minerals and vitamins.
- A peeled, quartered potato simmered in a salty soup for 15 minutes will absorb some of the excess salt.
- When storing broccoli, be sure that air can circulate all around it. If you store it in a tightly closed plastic bag, humidity will build up and decay will begin. Place it in a perforated plastic bag and refrigerate for up to 3 days.
- To core iceberg lettuce quickly and easily, simply slam the lettuce core side down on the counter, and the core will come out.
- Clean mushrooms when you are ready to eat them, with a soft brush or slightly damp cloth. If they are very dirty or gritty, rinse them in a colander under cold running water. Be sure to do it quickly so they don't absorb the water, since mushrooms are very porous.
- When steaming broccoli, lift the lid two or three times to allow the gases to escape. This

will also keep the color bright green. Or add a pinch of baking soda to the water to retain the bright green color.

- Odorless broccoli, cauliflower, or cabbage is easily obtained if you tear a slice of bread into small pieces and add it to the pot with the vegetables while they are cooking. The bread will absorb the odor.

- For easy tomato peeling, cut the core from the center of the tomato. Turn it over and score the bottom with an X. Drop the tomato into boiling water and simmer for ten seconds. Remove with a slotted spoon and drop into iced water. Cool 30 seconds and slide off the skin.

- Drop tablespoons of tomato paste into ice-cube trays, freeze until hard, and store in zip-type bags for up to 6 months for future use.

- Slice raw tomatoes vertically so that the inner pulp keeps and holds its shape for salads and doesn't turn into a mess.

- Vidalia onions have a very high moisture content and must be stored correctly. Place onions in panty hose and tie a knot after each onion. Cut off below the knot as each onion is needed. Make sure onions are stored in a cool, dry place, or wrap each onion separately in newspaper, paper towels, or aluminum foil and place in refrigerator. Raw or cooked onions may be stored in the freezer. The onions will lose some of their texture, but the flavor is just as good. Use for stews or soups.

- To roast garlic, cut off the pointed end of the

garlic bulb, then place the bulb on a piece of aluminum foil. Drizzle the garlic with olive oil, wrap it in foil, and then bake at 425°F. for 30 minutes. After it cools, squeeze the pulp from the bulb and spread on fresh Italian or French bread.

- To make garlic salt, put 3 peeled garlic cloves in 1/2 cup of salt. If desired, add freshly ground pepper and ground ginger to taste. Allow to stand for a few days in a closed container. Discard the garlic and use the salt as desired.

- Fresh garlic can be frozen. Chop or mince garlic and wrap in plastic wrap. Thaw only what you need. Unpeeled garlic heads and cloves can also be frozen. Place in an airtight container.

- Rub the inside or bottom of your salad bowl or fondue pot with a crushed garlic clove to add flavor.

- To peel a clove of garlic quickly, place a large clove flat on top of the stove, then smack it with a knife or the heel of your hand. The skin will crack, making it easier to peel.

- Mince garlic with ease by placing a peeled clove in a plastic zip-type bag and pounding it with a meat mallet. This will crush the garlic. Use in any recipe calling for minced garlic.

- Keep lettuces and other greens in a plastic bag or container in the crisper drawer of your refrigerator. Before using, separate and wash the leaves, or soak leaves in ice water for 10 to 20 minutes. To remove excess water, whirl the leaves in a salad spinner or pat dry gently with paper towels. Just before serving, tear leaves into small pieces and add salad dressing, toss, and serve. Never add salad dressing too far in advance, because the lettuce will soak it up and lose its crispness.

- Faster salad preparation is easy when you wash and dry your salad greens the night before. Then wrap the salad in a double thickness of paper towels and place in a plastic bag in your refrigerator.
- Tear, rather than cut, lettuce into pieces. Using a knife when cutting lettuce discolors the edges.
- Do not store lettuce with apples, pears, cantaloupe, or other foods that give off ethylene gas, which produces russet spots.
- To store asparagus, wrap the stems in a wet paper towel and place in a plastic bag, or stand them up with the ends in a little water.
- To save time when entertaining, prepare your vegetables the night before. Wash, dry, and slice or cut up your favorite vegetables and place in separate plastic bags. When you are ready to cook, remove the vegetables and prepare as desired.
- To cook vegetables in a flash, slice or julienne into thin strips rather than larger chunks. Steam or sauté just until tender.
- Do not refrigerate potatoes, but store in a cool, dark, airy place. If you purchase potatoes in a plastic bag, be sure to take them out

of it; place them in a large brown paper bag and keep it folded over.

- To prevent raw potatoes from turning dark before cooking, submerge them in cold water until ready to cook.

- Raw vegetables are loaded with enzymes that if left unchecked can cause the vegetables to discolor and soften even in the freezer. Blanching the vegetables before freezing them inactivates these enzymes.

- Kale makes both a beautiful garnish and a great addition to your centerpiece.

- Before cutting a scallion crosswise, make one vertical slit all the way from the root to the tip. This will double the number of scallion pieces produced.

- To pit an avocado, hold it on its side and slice around the pit, cutting full circle. Remove the knife and give the avocado a twist. The avocado will pull apart into two halves. To remove the pit, hit the top of it with the heel of a heavy knife. Give the knife a twist, turn, and lift. The pit will emerge stuck to the blade.

- To roast and peel peppers, place them under the broiler and turn often until they are broiled on all sides. Transfer the peppers into a paper or plastic bag, close, and set aside until cool (15 to 20 minutes). Halve and remove seeds. Lay halves flat and scrape or peel away any black bits of skin.

- To prolong the sweetness in raw onions, place chopped or diced onion in a strainer.

Dip several times into a bowl filled with water and a dash of vinegar. Drain the onion thoroughly. The acid in the vinegar prevents the onion from turning bitter.

- Do not discard carrots and celery after they have lost their crispness. Use them in soups and stews.
- Pack raw vegetables in a plastic bag for a healthy snack. Possibilities include carrot sticks or baby carrots, radishes, celery sticks, pepper slices, cauliflower, broccoli, and cherry tomatoes.
- Not all calcium comes from milk and cheese. Dark green leafy vegetables, including kale, turnip greens, collard greens, broccoli, and mustard greens, are excellent sources.
- For fast slicing and to ensure uniformity when slicing fresh mushrooms, use an egg slicer.
- For the fluffiest mashed potatoes, use a ricer.
- Rubbing potatoes with oil before baking will make their skins crispier.

2

Secrets About
the Seafood Department

Entering the seafood department can be a
daunting task for most shoppers, but in reality,
seafood is a great choice: delicious, versatile,
and healthy. The seafood department offers a
wide selection that is a natural for food in a
flash. The following tips will help you sort out
the seafood department, and armed with this
information you'll be ready to make a great
catch . . . and mealtime match!

Selecting Seafood

- The scales on fish should be shiny, not dull.
- If the fish is intact, the gills should be red in
  color.
- All fish should have a clean appearance and
  be firm to the touch.
- The fish should smell light without any heavy
  or fishy odor. This could indicate spoilage.
- Shrimp should be firm with shells tightly
  attached.
- If you are buying shrimp that have already

been shelled, be sure that they smell fresh
without a strong aroma.

- Lobsters should be alive. If you are purchasing cooked lobster, ask when it was
cooked to make sure that it is fresh.
- Oysters should be tightly closed; never buy
oysters with an open shell.
- All clams and mussels will close their shells
when tapped, so avoid those that do not
respond.
- Purchase seafood toward the end of your
shopping just as you do meat, chicken, or
milk. Ask the seafood manager the best way
to store each individual type of fish. Inquire
if it can be frozen, and if so, how to package
it. Get the facts!
- Get to know your seafood department
manager. Ask what his favorite choices for
the day are, and then for any cooking tips
he might suggest. Don't be scared to try
something new. You'll never know what
you're missing and it might be absolutely
delicious.

How Much Seafood per Person?

Fish
- *Whole fish:* 1 pound per person
- *Dressed/cleaned fish:* 3/4 pound per person
- *Fillets and steaks:* 1/3 to 1/2 pound per
person

Shellfish

- *Shellfish meat:* 1/3 to 1/2 pound per person
- *Live lobster, crab, crayfish:* 1 1/4 to 1 1/2 pounds per person
- *Live mussels or clams:* 2 to 3 pounds per person
- *Shrimp:* 1/2 pound per person

Cooking Times

- *Fish:* Cook for 8 to 10 minutes per inch of thickness for any cooking method except microwave (bake, broil, grill, fry, poach).
- *Whole crabs:* Boil 5 minutes per pound; steam whole crabs 10 minutes per pound.
- Be sure to check that any fish is fully cooked. Timing may vary, depending on cooking conditions.

Seafood Tips

- Avoid cross-contaminating cooked seafood with uncooked seafood. Use separate cutting boards, dishes, and utensils for raw and uncooked fish.
- To remove sand from clams, soak them in a large bowl of cold water with 2 teaspoons of salt and 2 teaspoons of cornmeal.
- Cook all seafood to an internal temperature of 145° F.
- Purchase seafood last and bring it home

as soon as possible. Better yet, keep a cooler in your car to place seafood in while transporting.

- What to look for? Buy seafood that smells, looks, and feels good.
- Refrigerate live shellfish in a ventilated container covered with a dampened towel or wrap it in a damp newspaper.
- Use fresh fish within a day or two and store at between 32° F. and 35° F. If it will be held longer than a day or two before consumption, freeze fish at 0° F. and use it within 6 months. Never refreeze thawed fish.
- Do not place oysters in a closed plastic bag; they will suffocate. Store the oysters in the refrigerator in a container loosely covered with clean, damp cloths. Oysters need to breathe.
- To make steamed or boiled shrimp go further, peel, devein, and cook the shrimp and then slice them in half lengthwise.
- Avoid overcooking shrimp by placing them in an ice bath immediately after they have been cooked to stop the cooking process.
- Cooking fish in parchment paper is a great low-fat cooking technique.
- Wash seafood in cold running water before preparing.
- Clams, oysters, and mussels should be live with shells that are tightly closed or close when handled.
- Leftover seafood should be refrigerated

immediately. Place it in shallow, nonabsorbent containers.

- Thaw seafood overnight in the refrigerator.
- If your fish is sliding around the work surface, try setting it on a paper towel to steady it. This works well for both a whole fish and fish pieces.
- When grilling fish, oil the grill and let it get hot before you place the fish on. For extra flavor, add water-soaked and drained wood chips to your charcoal or gas grill.
- Cook seafood over a moderately hot fire, but not too hot or the fish will char.
- Capers are often paired with seafood, but what are they? They are tiny green flower buds of a shrub native to the Mediterranean area and Asia. The buds are pickled in a vinegar brine. Tiny capers, or nonpareils, from France are considered the finest. The larger varieties are less expensive but just as tasty.
- To devein shrimp, first remove the shell (if desired, you may leave the tail intact). Using a small knife, make a shallow slit down the center of the outside of the shrimp. Remove the dark vein, then rinse the shrimp under cold water.
- To keep lobster tails straight while cooking, insert a bamboo skewer through the back of the tail and out the front. Remove the skewer when the lobster is cooked and the tail will stay straight.
- Even top-quality backfin crabmeat should be picked through for shell prior to use.

Tips for Cooking It Quick

- The smaller the pieces, the faster they cook. When time is critical, choose thinner fillets or cut thick fillets into cubes.
- When baking thin fillets or smaller pieces, turn up the heat to 425° F. for faster cooking.
- To prevent broiled fish from sticking, lightly oil the pan.
- Sauté fish over medium-high heat.
- Use seafood cubes, shrimp, scallops, or surimi in super-fast stir-fries.
- Seafood is a great choice for grilling: not only is it fast, but cleanup is a breeze. Cook your seafood and veggies by alternating on a skewer. Put shrimp and cubes of French bread on skewers, rub with garlic and olive oil, and then grill and place on your Caesar salad.

Seasonal Suggestions*

Spring
- Catfish
- Halibut
- Red snapper
- Salmon
- Blue crab
- Dungeness crab
- King crab
- Snow crab
- Lobster
- Shrimp

*Selection may vary depending on area.

Summer
- Bluefish
- Catfish
- Grouper
- Halibut
- Hawaiian ahi
- Red snapper
- Salmon
- Swordfish
- Tuna
- Bay scallops
- Lobster

Fall
- Catfish
- Orange roughy
- Salmon
- Tilapia
- Trout
- Clams
- Lobster
- Mussels
- Oysters
- Bay scallops
- Sea scallops
- Squid

Winter
- Catfish
- Cod
- Mahimahi
- Sea bass
- Tilapia
- Crab
- Mussels
- Shrimp

3

Secrets About
the Meat Department

Today's consumers are more health conscious than ever before. Fortunately the meat and poultry producers are listening! Beef and poultry are easy to prepare, and with improved labeling and more cooking information available to consumers, it's easier than ever to choose the right type of beef or poultry for your family.

The following tips will help you make better decisions when purchasing any type of meat. They will also assist you in making sure your meat stays fresh and is tasty.

Selecting Meat and Poultry

- When shopping for meat or poultry, be sure to inspect it and check all dates.
- Make sure the wrapper is sealed and there are no open areas or punctures in the packaging.
- The color of the meat and poultry should indicate freshness, with no discoloration or brown areas.
- Pick up meat and poultry items near the end of

your shopping and put them in the refrigerator as soon as you get home. If for some reason you are not going directly home or you have a long trip, bring along an ice-filled cooler and ask the meat manager for any safety precautions or packaging recommendations.

- Use meat or poultry within the food safety guidelines or freeze it immediately.
- When possible, place meat or poultry in plastic bags to keep the packages from dripping on the other food in your cart.
- Use beef steaks and roasts and poultry within three to four days. Use ground meat and ground poultry within one to two days.
- Get the facts! Don't be shy; talk to your meat manager regularly. Understand the labels and dates and know what you are purchasing. Get educated!

Poultry Tips

- Choose fresh chicken and turkey products, whether prepared or raw, that are clean, cold, wrapped well, sealed tight without rips or leaks, and sold from a refrigerated poultry case.
- Look for frozen poultry selections that are clean, packaged well, and rock solid to the touch.
- Check the safe handling label required on every poultry package.
- Don't open the package until you are ready to

cook the product. You should overwrap the package or put it on a plate to prevent meat juices from touching other foods.

- If you're watching calories, remove the skin from chicken breasts and poach the breasts in a small amount of chicken broth.
- You can substitute ground turkey for ground beef in casseroles, meat loaves, chili, or almost any recipe calling for ground beef.
- Don't throw out the chicken carcass. Use it as the foundation for your chicken stock.
- Cook white meat and bone-in chicken and turkey parts until juices are clear and the meat reaches an internal temperature of 170° F. on a meat thermometer. Dark meat should register 180° F. Boneless, skinless products should reach 160° F.
- When pounding chicken breasts, place them between layers of plastic wrap or in a heavy-duty zip-type bag. This will make your job easier and assist in cleanup duties.

Beef Tips

- Buy lean cuts of meat and trim away any visible fat.
- Cook stews, spaghetti sauces, chili, and soups that are made with beef a day in advance so that the flavors have a chance to meld.
- Select beef that is a bright cherry color, without any gray or brown blotches.
- Look for beef that is firm to the touch.

- To make cutting strips for stir-frying easier, partially freeze beef or chicken until the meat is firm.
- Use a gentle touch with ground beef. Over-mixing or compacting ground meats will result in dense burgers, meatballs, or meat loaves when cooked.
- Salt beef *after* cooking or browning. Salt draws out moisture and inhibits browning.
- Pat beef steaks, cubes, and pot roasts dry with paper toweling for better browning. This keeps grease from splattering as well.
- Never crowd beef in a pan when browning it or the meat will stew rather than brown.
- Leave a thin layer of fat on steaks and roasts during cooking to preserve juiciness. Trim the fat after cooking.
- Nonstick cookware surfaces are easier to clean and allow cooking with less fat. Aluminum and cast iron are reactive metals; they can affect the taste and color of dishes that contain acidic ingredients.
- Always marinate foods in the refrigerator, never at room temperature.
- Tender beef cuts need to be marinated only 15 minutes to 2 hours for flavor.
- Marinating meat longer than 24 hours in a tenderizing marinade can result in a mushy texture.
- If a marinade is to be used later for basting or served as a sauce, reserve a portion of it before adding beef or chicken.
- Never save or reuse a marinade!

- Allow 1/4 to 1/2 cup of marinade for each 1 to 2 pounds of beef.
- For easy marinating, after mixing the substance, place it in a sealed heavy-duty zip-type bag with your meat or chicken.
- High heat can overcook or char the outside of beef cuts while the inside remains underdone. For tender beef, cooked to the desired doneness, use medium heat with dry cookery methods and low heat for moist cookery methods.
- Turn steaks and roasts with tongs. Do not use a fork, which pierces the beef and allows flavorful juices to escape.
- Lemon juice is a natural tenderizer for beef.
- Turn ground beef patties with a spatula. Do not flatten them; this causes flavorful juices to escape, resulting in a drier burger.
- For roasts, use a meat thermometer. There are two types to choose from. An ovenproof meat thermometer is inserted prior to roasting and left in the entire time. An instant-read thermometer is not ovenproof. Use this toward the end of recommended cooking time. Insert it long enough to get a temperature reading (about 10 to 15 seconds), then remove it.
- Divide leftovers into small portions to speed chilling or freezing and, later, defrosting.
- To remove the fat from any stock (homemade or canned), simply refrigerate the stock in a large bowl overnight. When the stock has

gelled, remove all the solidified fat from the surface.

- To keep beef cut for frying or bacon from curling, snip the edges with shears before cooking.

- To keep beef cut for frying or bacon on hand, roll each strip up and store them in a zip-type bag for future use.

- When making a meal ahead of time, once you cook meat or poultry, never leave it on the counter until dinner. Let it cool for 10 to 15 minutes and then refrigerate. If you are setting the table, cook and put the meat out last.

- Avoid letting meat or poultry sit on a buffet for even a few hours. It's better to refill a tray than to let it spoil. This also saves having to throw out the leftovers from buffet dinners that have been sitting out too long.

4

Secrets About
the Dairy Department

Fresh from the farm to a grocer near you, eggs, milk, cheese, and butter are products that we all use daily and think we know everything about. Or do we? Dairy products should be purchased with care. There are many simple secrets about your dairy products that you will benefit from knowing. The following tips may help you avoid another trip back to the grocery or farmers' market with an expired or spoiled product. Read on and learn more!

Selecting Dairy Products

- The dairy department is an area where you need to be aware of expiration dates and freshness. Inspect all packages and don't assume anything!
- Open the egg carton and check for broken or cracked eggs. If you see any cracks, even small ones, do not purchase.
- If possible, lift the lid on products such as sour cream, cream cheese, or yogurt to see if

the clear plastic cover under the lid is intact. Bacteria can grow under an open seal.

- Some cheeses are highly perishable and should be used within a few days. Check to see if there is an expiration date on the package, or inquire what it is if you are in doubt.
- Check the date on your milk before purchasing it. Look to the back of the dairy shelf to see if there are any later dates.

More Tips About Eggs

- Always buy refrigerated grade A or AA eggs with clean, uncracked shells. If any eggs crack on the way home, discard them.
- There is no difference between brown and white eggs as far as content is concerned. The color of the shell is determined by the breed of hen that lays them.
- Always refrigerate eggs immediately, storing them in their original egg cartons.
- To test an egg for freshness, place it in a bowl of cold water. A fresh egg will remain on the bottom, while an older egg will float slightly. Discard any egg that floats on the surface.
- To tell a hard-boiled egg from one that is raw, simply spin the egg. The raw egg will not spin, while the hard-boiled egg will.
- To hard-boil eggs easily, begin with eggs that are at room temperature. In a pot large enough to hold the eggs in a single layer, bring cold water to a boil. When the water is boiling,

place the eggs in the pot carefully. This can be done with a spoon. Boil 8 minutes for small eggs and 10 minutes for large ones. Remove eggs from the heat and cool them immediately in several changes of cold water. Eggs are easier to separate from their shells if they are cold.

- To prevent stuffed hard-cooked eggs from sliding around on the plate, anchor each in place with a tiny dab of stuffing.
- To hold eggs together while poaching them, add a few drops of vinegar or lemon juice to the cooking water.
- Beat egg whites right before you need them. If beaten egg whites are not used immediately, the air beaten into them escapes and they become watery.
- Egg whites will beat best when they are at room temperature. After slightly beating the whites, add a pinch of salt or cream of tartar to help them stiffen.
- To bring eggs to room temperature quickly, put them in a bowl of warm water for 5 to 10 minutes.

More Tips About Cheese

- Cheese makes a great beginning or ending to meals. Serve a well-balanced variety at room temperature. Allow 1/4 pound per person. Choose one cheese from each category: soft ripening (such as Brie), semisoft (Port-Salut

or Monterey Jack), firm (Swiss or cheddar), and blue-veined (blue or Stilton).
- Before grating or shredding cheese, lightly oil the cheese grater for easy cleanup.
- For shavings of Parmesan cheese, push a swivel-blade vegetable peeler across a large, flat piece of Parmesan cheese, letting the shavings fall directly onto the food that is to be garnished.
- Hard cheeses such as Parmesan can be frozen without losing any of their character.
- To soften cream cheese easily without melting it, place it in a zip-type bag and immerse the bag in hot water. In a matter of minutes your cheese will be soft and pliable.
- When cooking with cheese, remember: slow and low! Cooking too long or fast will result in oily or rubbery cheese.
- A pinch of dry mustard added to cheese sauces accents the taste.

More Tips About Butter

- Salted butter will keep for several weeks in its original package in the coldest part of the refrigerator. Butter freezes well up to one month in its original package and up to nine months in freezer paper.
- To clarify butter, melt 1 pound of butter over low heat in a heavy pan. Skim off the froth and carefully pour the clear yellow liquid

into a container, leaving the milky residue behind. Discard this residue.

- For a thin slice of butter that will melt easily, use your cheese slicer for slicing. This is great for spreading butter on bagels or toast.
- To make flavored butter, mix softened butter with your choice of herbs, spices, or nuts. Use it for basting or grilling or on hot bread.

More Tips About Milk and Cream

- Always check expiration dates before purchasing milk and cream products.
- Under optimum conditions, milk will last beyond the expiration date. Optimum conditions include maintaining your refrigerator at the recommended 45° F.
- Be sure to refrigerate your milk and cream purchases as soon as possible.
- Never leave your milk container out on the table while having your meal. Instead, place only the amount you'll need in a carafe and leave the container in the refrigerator. This factors into its prolonged freshness.
- When whipping cream, be sure that the bowl, heavy cream, and beaters are very cold. You can also add a pinch of salt to the cream before whipping to strengthen the fat and make the cream thicken faster.

5

Secrets About Oils and Vinegars

Oils and vinegars are something of a mystery to many cooks. They can be used in lots of ways, so it's important to know how to use them. There are many different kinds of oils and vinegars, and when used properly they can be a fabulous asset to any meal. Not only do they flavor food, but they also can improve the actual cooking experience. The following tips will help you on your way down the oil and vinegar aisle.

Selecting Oils and Vinegars

- Read the labels on the bottle. Many oils and vinegars will tell you exactly what they are good for and how to use them.
- Try something new. Don't be reluctant to experiment. Ask your grocer or a food expert at the store which ones he or she has tried. You'll be surprised at what you learn!
- Compare labels when choosing between two oils. Figure out which one is the healthier choice.

Types of Olive Oil

- Extra virgin olive oil is always made from the first pressing of the olives. It has an intense aroma and flavor that is best used for drizzling over salads, roasted vegetables, pasta, or whenever its particular flavor is important. It is best to store olive oil in a cool, dark place away from the sun's harmful ultraviolet rays. Olive oil that is stored properly will last for up to 6 months.
- Virgin olive oil is produced from the second pressing of the olives, resulting in a slightly sweet, fruity flavor.
- Pure olive oil consists of oils extracted from the previously pressed olive pulp.
- Fine olive oil is also produced from previously pressed olive oil pulp, but it contains added water. Because of its very high acidity, it is perfect for sautéing or frying.

More Tips for Using Olive Oil

- To keep calories down when using olive oil for your salads, place your favorite oil in a plastic spray bottle and lightly spritz your salad, grill, and broiling pan. This trick also works well for your chicken, fish, beef, and vegetables when grilling.
- When grilling or broiling meats and chicken, brush the meat with olive oil to seal in juices.

- Toss fresh vegetables in olive oil with garlic and grill or roast.
- Use olive oil for stir-frying or sautéing.
- Rub baked potatoes with olive oil and salt before baking for added crispiness.
- You can make croutons by sprinkling French bread with olive oil, black pepper, garlic, and Parmesan. Bake them at 400° F. until they appear golden brown.
- Keep olive oil on your table to add to stews, soups, salads, and pastas.
- Use olive oil for your bread instead of butter or margarine.
- Dip raw vegetables into olive oil flavored with ground black pepper.

Commonly Used Oils

- *Corn oil:* Widely available in supermarkets, this unsaturated oil is perfect for frying. It is also a popular choice for low-cholesterol diets because it contains no cholesterol. This type of oil can be stored in a cool, dark place for up to 6 months or refrigerated for up to a year.
- *Peanut oil:* Popular in Chinese cooking, this oil imparts a slight peanut flavor and is perfect for stir-fries and high-heat frying. Peanut oil will keep for a year in a cool, dark place.
- *Safflower oil:* A good choice for making infused oils. It has no flavor and will not interfere with other seasonings. It is also

excellent for high frying temperatures and will keep for up to a year in a cool, dark place.

- *Sesame oil:* Pressed from sesame seeds, this oil is often recommended for Chinese cooking, stir-fries, dipping sauces, soups, and Asian noodle dishes. It can be stored for up to 6 months in a cool, dark place.

- *Soybean oil:* A good choice for special diets, this cholesterol-free oil is one of the most popular bland oils used for high-heat frying. It can be stored for up to a year in a cool, dark place.

- *Hazelnut oil and walnut oil:* These oils tend to be more expensive and are usually imported from France. Heating these oils often destroys their fine fragrance and special flavors. These are best drizzled over steamed or grilled vegetables and used in salad dressings and mayonnaise. They will keep up to one year when refrigerated.

More Tips About Vinegar

- The variety of vinegars available to consumers has increased dramatically in recent years. Today, well-stocked supermarkets offer an excellent array, including flavored vinegars. An important ingredient in salads, vinegar is also a terrific meat tenderizer when used in meat marinades.

- You can store vinegar in a cool, dry location for up to 6 months.

- Herbs may be added to vinegar for extra

flavor. Good choices are basil, tarragon, peppercorns, oregano, dill, rosemary, chives, and herbes de Provence.

- Standard vinaigrette is made up of 3 parts olive oil to 1 part vinegar (balsamic, red wine, or other).
- Cooked greens such as spinach and collards get an extra boost in flavor from vinegar. Put the vinegar directly in the cooking water.

Types of Vinegar

- *Wine vinegar:* Red or white wine vinegar is made by fermenting wine until it becomes sufficiently acidic. Red wine vinegar is generally used in marinades, vinaigrettes, salads, and salad dressings. White wine vinegar is best for pickling, fish, and potato salad.
- *Cider vinegar, or apple cider vinegar:* Made from the juice of apples, its mild, fruity tones can be used to make dressings or in pickling.
- *Raspberry vinegar:* Its raspberry flavor and aroma are best paired with chicken, fruit salads, duck, and fresh green salads.
- *Sherry vinegar:* A distinctive vinegar made from Spanish sherry, it is excellent in dressings, with asparagus, green beans, or salads, and for deglazing.
- *Rice vinegar:* A staple in Japanese and Chinese cooking, this is also an important component in Asian noodle dishes, salad dressings, dipping sauces, and soy sauce.

6

Secrets About
Herbs, Spices, and Nuts

Herbs play an important role in cooking. After
all, the flavors and aromas of dishes depend
very much on herbs and spices. When you
want to accent and enhance your meal, reach
for herbs. Nuts also play a variety of roles in
the kitchen, from appetizers to trail mix, gra-
nola to salads, rice dishes and cooked vegetables to breads and desserts. Read on to find
helpful tips and information for this versatile
ingredient. In fact, with all these new uses
you're bound to go nuts!

Selecting Herbs, Spices, and Nuts

- Buy herbs and spices in small amounts, as
  their flavor and strength diminish with time.
- Ask your grocer for recommendations about
  which herbs and spices to use with a specific
  recipe. Check your recipe books for additional hints. Learn what goes with what.
- Stock up on spices that you see recommended often in your favorite cookbooks.

Before you know it, you'll know how to use them appropriately.

- Unless you plan to use nuts in a recipe or snack within a reasonable amount of time, it is better to freeze them.
- When you get home from shopping, store your dried spices away from light and heat.

More Tips About Herbs and Spices

- Whenever possible, use fresh herbs. You can really taste the difference. Also, fresh herbs make a beautiful garnish for foods, cheese trays, and even desserts. All of these could benefit from sharing a plate with a fresh mint garnish.
- Keeping herbs fresh is so simple, yet so important. First, trim the ends of the herbs with scissors. Next, place the entire bunch in a glass half filled with water, then cover the glass with a plastic bag and refrigerate. Basil, cilantro, watercress, and parsley benefit the most from this treatment.
- To keep fresh herbs on hand year-round, try chopping the herbs and putting 1 tablespoon of chopped herbs into each cube section of an ice tray. Add a little water and freeze. When you need fresh herbs, simply remove the desired amount, thaw, drain, blot dry, and add them to your favorite recipe.
- You can also add fresh sprigs of herbs to your summer flower bouquets. A bouquet of herbs

from your garden or grocer makes a lovely, fragrant centerpiece.

- Fresh herbs also make a great gift for your favorite cook. Select an assortment of small herbs and place them in a basket, or plant them in an attractive planter. Many herbs will grow for years to come.

- A small electric coffee grinder is great for pulverizing whole spices. Reserve it for spices only and use a separate grinder for your coffee.

- Plant a shallot in a small pot filled with soil to keep on your kitchen counter. In approximately a week or so, you will have great-tasting chives ready to be snipped when needed.

- Simple-to-make herb mayonnaise is great for sandwiches, as a topping for fish or chicken, served on the side as a spread, and in potato and egg salads. Combine 1 cup of mayonnaise (can be nonfat or low-fat) and 2 tablespoons of chopped fresh basil, thyme, chives, etc. Refrigerate for 1 hour before using. Refrigerated, your special mayonnaise will last for up to 1 week.

- Herb-flavored butters can be made from fresh or dried herbs. Cream 1/2 cup of butter and add minced chives, parsley, paprika, garlic, shallots, or tarragon. Season to taste, place in a small serving bowl or roll into a log in plastic wrap, and refrigerate until ready to use. Flavored butters may also be frozen. These are fantastic on grilled fish, chicken, meat, vegetables, and of course, warm crusty bread.

- Parsley makes a great natural breath freshener when chewed.
- *Bouquet garni:* This classic French herb assortment is used for stews, soups, and stocks. You can make your own supply by tying parsley, thyme, and bay leaves together and then tying the string to the pot handle so that it can be easily removed at the end of the cooking time.
- *Herbes de Provence:* This is a blend of dried herbs typical of Provence—thyme, rosemary, marjoram, basil, fennel, and mint. Use in stews and vegetable dishes.
- *Fines herbes:* These are traditionally French and consist of finely chopped subtle herbs such as parsley, tarragon, chervil, and chives. They are excellent for flavoring omelets, egg dishes, chicken, vegetable dishes, and poached fish.
- Spice rubs are a great way to add flavors to meat, poultry, and fish before cooking without adding extra fat. Combine equal amounts of spices such as garlic, shredded lemon peel, dried crushed oregano, and salt and pepper. Rub the mixture over chicken breasts or fish. Cook as desired.
- Buy dried herbs in small amounts and keep them in a cool, dark location. If they are stored properly, they should last for approximately 6 months.
- When using dried instead of fresh herbs in any recipe, use half the amount the directions call for. Dried herbs are stronger.

- Fresh ginger can easily be peeled by scraping the skin off with a teaspoon.
- Always mince or chop herbs just before you use them. Flavors are quickly lost as volatile oils are released.
- Keep your pantry stocked with flavored mustards, spicy salsas, Chinese spices, and bottled marinades for a quick meal when there's no time to shop. Timesaving flavor-boosters can make a meal quick and easy.

More Tips About Nuts

- When selecting nuts, remember that unshelled nuts should feel heavy for their size.
- Heat, light, and moisture can cause nuts to go rancid quickly. Store whole nuts in their shell for up to 6 months, or freeze them for up to a year. Shelled nuts should also be refrigerated or frozen.
- Toasting brings out the full flavor of nuts. Spread whole, chopped, or sliced nuts in a thin layer on a baking sheet. Bake the nuts at 350° F. for 5 to 10 minutes or until they are a light golden brown, shaking the sheet occasionally. Keep a close watch on them because they burn easily. Also, sliced or chopped nuts brown quicker than whole nuts.
- Peanut butter will stay fresher longer if you store it in the refrigerator.
- Nuts have a high fat content, so they can quickly turn to paste during grinding. When

you are grinding nuts in a food processor, it is best to mix them with a little sugar or any flour called for in the recipe.

- Top your casseroles with crushed nuts for an extra crunch that's really tasty.
- The following nuts are fabulous for stir-fries: almonds, cashews, macadamias, peanuts, and walnuts.
- The following nuts are great for baking: almonds, hazelnuts, pecans, pine nuts (pignolia), pistachios, and walnuts.
- The following nuts are suggested for snack mixes: almonds, cashews, macadamias, peanuts, pecans, pistachios, and walnuts.

7

Secrets About
Coffee and Tea

Coffee and tea are enjoyed all over the world every day, and for good reason. Their soothing qualities and refreshing taste make them the perfect beverages for any time of the day and for every occasion. Perhaps you have experimented with the new blends and types of coffees and teas. If you have, then you have probably discovered that the choices are endless! They can also be quite challenging. The following tips will assist you in selecting and enjoying coffee and tea.

Purchasing Coffee and Tea

• Coffee and tea are perishable in the sense that their flavor is greatly reduced over time. Keep this in mind as you buy them.
• To avoid waste, try new kinds of coffee and tea in small packages or in samplers with a variety of choices. This way you can experiment without wasting a great deal of money.

More Tips About Coffee

- Specialty coffee beans (arabica) have half the caffeine of low-grade (robusta) coffee beans.
- When you buy a pound of coffee beans, you will be carrying in that little bag approximately the yearly output of 1 average coffee tree.
- One pound of coffee beans equals about 2,000 hand-picked coffee cherries.
- Leftover coffee can be very useful. Pour it into an ice cube tray and freeze. The cubes can then be added to iced coffee. This will prevent iced coffee from being diluted.
- Did you know that since the Boston tea party, coffee has been America's drink? We consume more than half the world's coffee production.
- Begin your coffee brewing process with cold tap water. Cold tap water is purer than hot or warm water, which may contain sediment from your water heater.
- Stained coffee cups should be rinsed with vinegar and then gently rubbed with a cloth dipped in salt. Wash the cup in warm soapy water afterward, then rinse and dry.
- Coffee was brought to the New World (Martinique) in the early eighteenth century by a French naval officer named de Clue, who smuggled a few tiny plants on board his ship. These plants formed the basis of the coffee industry in the Caribbean and South America.
- A brewed 5-ounce cup of specialty coffee has

about 90 milligrams of caffeine. The decaffeinated version has about 2 milligrams. In comparison, a 5-ounce cup of hot cocoa has about 12 milligrams of caffeine and a 5-ounce cup of tea about 40 milligrams.

- Espresso is not a drink but a brewing method. Hot water under high pressure is forced through a bed of finely ground coffee to extract a thick, flavorful essence in a concentrated form. The extraction should take 18 to 25 seconds.

- All coffee is perishable. Its enemy: flavor-robbing air. Coffee should always be stored in an airtight, moisture-proof container. The container should always be placed in your refrigerator or your freezer—the colder the better.

- It takes 4 to 5 years for a coffee tree to start producing fruit (green berries). When the berries turn red and ripe, they are picked. Two coffee beans are contained in each berry. An experienced picker can harvest some 200 pounds of berries a day, enough to produce about 24 pounds of coffee.

- Brew either hazelnut- or banana-split-flavored coffee to full strength (add an extra 2 scoops to your pot). Add ¾ ounce of chocolate syrup to 4 ounces of brewed coffee and mix. Fill the remainder of your mug with heated milk. For a nominal cost you have just made yourself an expensive coffeehouse drink!

- For an afternoon pick-me-up or after-dinner beverage, why not try adding a spoonful of vanilla ice cream or whipped cream to your favorite brewed flavored coffee?

- Try using honey instead of sugar in coffee and tea.

More Tips About Tea

Making the Perfect Cup of Tea

1. Always use the best tea that you can afford.
2. Fill the kettle with cold tap water; hot or reheated water contains less dissolved air and has a flat, stale taste.
3. Warm the teapot by rinsing it out with hot water.
4. Add 1 teaspoon of tea or 1 tea bag per person and also 1 for the pot (or 1 teaspoon for every 6 fluid ounces).
5. When the water is boiling, pour the water into the teapot. Replace the lid and let the tea infuse for about 5 minutes (remember, large leaves take longer to brew than smaller ones). After you have allowed the tea to infuse, if it is too strong for your liking, use less tea next time.
6. Serve the tea immediately. Never hold a pot of brewed tea for more than 10 minutes or it will turn bitter.

- Always use the same care to prepare tea properly even when using a tea bag. Allow the tea time to infuse and release its flavor. Never simply dip a tea bag.

- Tea should be stored in an airtight container to preserve its freshness.
- Avoid using detergent or soap when washing a teapot, because the lingering sediment can spoil the taste of the tea.

Secrets About
the Deli Department

The deli department is more popular than ever. This is the spot for consumers' fast-paced lifestyles. Deli meats, cheeses, prepared salads, and rotisserie chickens can cut the preparation time for meals down to minutes. But how do you purchase deli so that it stays fresh? How long should you keep it? These questions deserve answers.

The tips in this chapter will help you when you visit the deli department. But don't be shy—the deli managers in most grocery stores, delis, or farmers' markets are ready and waiting to help you with any information you need or want to know!

Selecting Items from the Deli Department

- Ask for a sample. When in doubt, ask to taste it! This works especially well when your children are with you and you want to make sure they like something. Most grocery stores are happy to offer you a sample!
- Ask to see the label and feel free to request

specific information. While deli items are purchased in bulk, they still have labeling on the package. Compare the salt content, ingredients—you name it! Often this will help you make your decision.

- Request packaging the way you like it. Some shoppers prefer their deli purchases split in half to keep them fresh when they are stored in the refrigerator. If a package is left open by accident, the entire purchase can be spoiled. Another possibility is to transfer part of your purchase into plastic wrap and then put that into another sealable bag.
- Inquire how long the deli item is good for. Get the facts about your purchase and make sure you transfer the date if you are repackaging your deli purchase. Avoid tearing off the date when opening the package.

More Tips About the Deli

- Refrigerate your deli items as soon as possible after making your purchase.
- Remove the deli meats from their original wrappers and rewrap them in plastic wrap. Then place each package in a zip-type bag. This helps the product last longer.
- Leave only the amount of meat out on the counter that you will be using to make sandwiches.

Deli Storage Tips

Storage times are based on the date of purchase and may vary depending on product. Always discard any food that is showing signs of spoilage or has an odor.

- *Deli foods (entrées hot or cold):* 3 to 4 days, or 2 to 3 months if frozen
- *Sliced lunch meats:* 3 to 5 days, or 1 to 2 months if frozen
- *Salads:* 3 to 5 days (do not freeze)
- *Bacon:* 7 days (after the package has been opened), or 1 month if frozen
- *Hot dogs sealed in package:* 2 weeks, or 1 to 2 months if frozen
- *Hot dogs after opening:* 1 week, or 1 to 2 months if frozen
- *Smoked or processed lunch meats sealed in package:* 2 weeks, or 1 to 2 months if frozen
- *Smoked or processed lunch meats after opening:* 3 to 5 days, or 1 to 2 months if frozen
- *Cooked or processed poultry lunch meats sealed in the package:* 2 weeks, or 1 to 2 months if frozen
- *Cooked or processed poultry lunch meats after opening:* 3 to 5 days, or 1 to 2 months if frozen
- *Rotisserie chicken:* 3 to 4 days, or 4 months if frozen
- *Smoked fish:* 14 days, or follow the date on the vacuum package

- *Sliced hard salami or pepperoni:* 2 to 3 weeks, or 1 to 2 months if frozen

Deli Sandwich Tips

- Most cold sandwiches can be made ahead of time. Make sure that they are wrapped properly and stored in the refrigerator. However, if you are making a very wet sandwich or one that has tomatoes and pickles, wait to make it until you are ready to eat. Otherwise, these ingredients tend to soak through the bread. You could also wrap the wet ingredients separately. Also, a slight disadvantage to making sandwiches ahead of time is that bread goes stale faster under refrigeration than at room temperature.
- Place sandwiches in the top half of your cooler so they will stay cold and will not be crushed under your drinks or condiments.
- When making sandwiches for a large party or picnic, try the assembly-line approach. Lay out all the deli items, cheeses, condiments, and bread slices. Use a spatula for spreading mayonnaise and mustard to enable you to work faster.
- When slicing cheese for sandwiches, use a cheese parer rather than a knife.
- Here are some suggested cheeses for your deli sandwiches: cheddar, Swiss, mozzarella, Jarlsberg, Muenster, Gouda, fontina, Brie, havarti, and garlic cheese spreads.

- You can add zip to your sandwiches with flavored mayonnaise.
- Deli sausages such as knockwurst are great when tossed in salads.
- Smoked fish is terrific for every occasion.

Other Items Available from the Deli Counter

- *Sturgeon:* The crème de la crème of smoked fish is expensive yet worth the money.
- *Sable:* This American saltwater fish has a firm, white, flaky texture.
- *Whitefish:* This fish is smoked until golden, has a firm, sweet, and full flavor, and is perfect for the buffet table, for sandwiches on challah bread, or as a fabulous spread.
- *Carp:* This fish makes a great appetizer.
- *Chubs:* These are similar to whitefish in taste, but are usually less expensive.
- *Baked salmon:* A favorite for any occasion, salmon is best paired with potato salad.
- *Kipper:* These are actually herring. Plan on one per person. If the kippers are very small, you should plan on two per person.
- *Herring:* This fish has a distinctive smoky flavor and aroma.
- *Nova:* Moist, tender, and delicious when paired with onions, capers, and dill, nova can be served as an appetizer or an entrée.
- *Lox:* This is similar in taste to nova but is much saltier.

9

Secrets About
Pasta and Rice

Pasta and rice have long been staples for half
of the world's population. Always a favorite
and always delicious, what could be faster or
more versatile to have on hand? From a quick
dinner to a fast side dish, pasta and rice are
perfect choices for last-minute meals. Because
there are so many varieties of pasta and rice,
the possibilities are truly endless. Pasta and
rice are the perfect foods for entertaining and
can really help stretch your budget. Be sure to
keep both on hand for a fast, satisfying meal in
minutes. The following tips will help you as
you stock up.

Purchasing Pasta and Rice

• Always inspect the package your pasta or
  rice comes in. Look at the expiration date
  and also the contents. Make certain that
  the package hasn't been damaged or opened,
  and that the contents are fresh and appear
  safe from tampering.

- Factory-made pasta is made from semolina; the various shapes are obtained by extruding the dough, which is then dried. Certain cuts of pasta are better suited to certain dishes. Follow the recipe or read the package.
- When you store pasta or rice, be sure to rotate both to keep them fresh. Also, check these items often to make sure they are closed and free of any problems.

More Tips About Pasta

- The secret to cooking pasta perfectly is to use a large pot with plenty of water.
- Salting the pasta water is not always necessary, so if you are watching your salt intake, you can leave the salt out completely. If you prefer salt, simply add 1 or 2 teaspoons to the pasta water and bring it to a boil.
- Always start with cold tap water when cooking pasta. Warm or hot water may contain sediment from your water heater.
- Before adding pasta to the water, wait until it has come to a full rolling boil, then gently add your favorite pasta. The rolling boil will keep your pasta moving and allow it to cook evenly.
- After cooking the pasta, drain it well. Otherwise the sauce will not coat the pasta properly and may become diluted from the extra water.
- A great timesaving technique is to cook your

pasta ahead of time and hold it until you are ready to add the sauce or other ingredients. Be sure to rinse the pasta and drain it well. It can then be reheated for a few minutes in the microwave. You can also reheat cooked pasta by reserving some of the hot cooking water in a container before completely draining the pasta; finish draining the pasta and return it to the pot. When you are ready to serve, add the hot cooking liquid back to the pot and stir and drain again. However, if you are cooking pasta for a cold pasta salad or the pasta will be reheated again, as in lasagne or baked ziti, drain the pasta well, then rinse it with cold water and drain again.

- Tossing cooked pasta with oil to prevent its sticking will add extra calories and can also prevent the sauce from adhering to the pasta.
- Wonton or egg-roll wrappers make excellent "handmade" ravioli in minutes. Prepare your favorite filling and place it in the center of one wrapper. Place a second wrapper on top and seal by pressing the edges closed. Boil until they float, and add your favorite sauce.
- Cooking times for pasta can vary according to shape and size, so be sure to follow package directions: remove a piece of the cooked pasta, rinse it under cold water, and taste it. If it is to your liking, remove the pasta from the heat and drain. If it is too firm, continue to cook for 1 to 2 minutes and test it again.
- For the pasta that will cook the quickest

when you are short on time, choose the thinner varieties such as angel hair, orzo, and other small shapes.

- Did you ever wonder how they make colored pasta? Colored pasta is made by adding tomato paste, spinach, herbs, carrots, beet juice, saffron, or even squid ink!

- Did you know that eating pasta, a complex carbohydrate, releases serotonin, a neurotransmitter in the brain?

- Which pasta is better, dried or fresh? It is purely a matter of individual taste.

- Add your leftover uncooked pasta to soups. Adding a few different varieties to soups and broth makes a unique and festive presentation.

- Save time in the kitchen by microwaving your sauce while your pasta is cooking.

- Microwaves are perfect for heating pasta dishes that were made earlier in the day, for reheating pasta leftovers, or for thawing frozen pasta casseroles.

- Pasta doesn't always mean Italian. Look for fun types of pasta in the Asian department of your grocery, too.

- When serving pasta from a large pasta bowl, always warm the bowl first by filling it with hot water, allowing it to stand, and then draining it just before filling it with the pasta.

- To reduce the fat content of your meat sauce, replace beef with chopped vegetables or ground chicken or turkey.

Pasta Pairings

- Penne (quill), fusilli (spirals), radiatore (little radiators), and farfalle (butterflies) are all shapes that are ideal for meat sauces, vegetable sauces, and salads.
- Rigatoni (grooved) and rotini (wheels) are perfect for baked dishes.
- Spaghetti, spaghettini, linguine, fettuccine, and capellini are all long shapes that work well with rich sauces and sauces that cling.

More Tips About Rice

- When using imported rice such as basmati, be sure to pick through and rinse before using.
- To prepare rice that doesn't stick together, try adding a little oil or butter in the pot and sautéing the rice slightly before adding the water.
- The microwave will save you time in cleanup and in keeping the kitchen cool, but it will not save you time in cooking rice. Rice requires the same amount of cooking time whether you cook it in the microwave or on the stove top.
- Resist the temptation to remove the pan lid to check your rice while it is cooking, and always fluff it with a fork before serving.

Converted Rice and Beyond

- Converted rice, also known as parboiled rice, has been steamed and dried prior to removal of the hull and bran. It's popular because it's easy to prepare and offers almost foolproof cooking. It's also a good all-purpose rice that adapts well to reheating and still maintains its quality.
- Both short-grain rice and medium-grain rice are moist, tender, and somewhat sticky. Short-grain rice is a favorite for sushi as well as rice puddings, molded rice rings, and croquettes.
- Basmati is a beautifully fragrant and aromatic long-grain rice. Basmati is grown in India and Pakistan. With its distinctively nutty flavor, it makes an unusual and distinctive side dish. It is also widely used in pilafs and curries.
- Arborio is grown in Italy's Po Valley and is a short-grain rice that is used for making risotto. Its high starch content results in its creamy texture. Arborio is a slow-cooked rice that requires constant stirring; it is usually cooked with broth rather than water. It makes a fabulous entrée and is definitely worth all the cooking attention that it requires.
- Instant rice is a precooked and dried rice. It is the rice to use when time is of the utmost importance, although the flavor and texture suffer somewhat.

- Wild rice is not a true rice, but a water grass usually grown in North American marshlands. It is a firm rice with a somewhat nutty flavor. It lends itself well to side dishes and soups as well as to cold rice salads mixed with nuts and dried fruit. Always rinse wild rice before cooking: simply place in a saucepan and cover with water, then scoop off any debris that floats to the top. Drain and then proceed with the recipe.

- Brown rice is an unpolished rice that retains its valuable bran. Brown rice takes longer to cook than white, but the additional nutrients are well worth it. With its dense, nutty flavor and texture, it is a wonderful rice for salads. Take care not to overcook.

10

Secrets About the Bakery Department

The bakery is the department in the grocery store where freshness counts most! Nothing tastes worse than dry bread or stale pastries. The following tips will not only help you to make the most of your purchases in this department but also teach you how to maximize and extend the life of even stale bread! Bakery products can and should be put to creative use, and often your presentation is the key. You can turn breads into fabulous centerpieces for dips and learn how to cut cheesecake like the pros. Sweet tooths, unite, this chapter was written with you in mind!

Selecting Baked Goods

- All bakery items are very perishable, so be sure to check dates.
- If a date isn't clearly visible, don't hesitate to ask the bakery department manager how fresh the item is.
- Check out which items freeze well before

64

buying them for a later date. Some things are best when eaten fresh.

- A tiny perforation or a box with open sides will make your bakery items dry out faster and taste stale. For a fresher taste, repackage any items that aren't being eaten immediately, and watch what you buy.

More Tips About the Bakery

- If you have bought bread that you do not plan to use immediately, place it in a plastic resealable storage bag to maintain freshness.
- Hollow out a small round loaf of bread for a great soup bowl.
- Turn your leftover bread into bread crumbs. First remove the bottom crust. Next, cut the bread into cubes and place them in your food processor. Process to the desired size. If you are making bread crumbs for immediate use, toast them lightly on a baking sheet. Otherwise, store them in a zip-type bag in your freezer. They will last for up to 1 month.
- Croutons are easily made from leftover bread. Cut the bread into small cubes, spray or toss lightly with your favorite oil, and bake at 375° F. until golden brown. If desired, season with garlic, salt, pepper, and Parmesan or your favorite herbs.
- *Garlic bread:* To prevent breaking or tearing your bread, rub a peeled garlic clove on the

crusty edges only. The rough texture of the crust grates the garlic and flavors the slice.

- Before freezing fresh bagels, cut them in half. They will defrost faster and you will avoid having to slice a frozen bagel.
- To slice bread easily, use a hot knife.
- When slicing an ice cream cake, use a knife dipped in hot water for a neat, clean cut.
- A cake will stay fresh days longer if an apple, cut in half, is stored with the cake.
- The best slicing technique for creamy cheesecake is to use unflavored dental floss. Simply cut a piece of dental floss several inches longer than the cake's diameter. Holding the floss taut, set the floss on top of the cake. Press down, pushing through to the bottom of the cake. Let go of one end of the floss and pull it through to the other side.
- Turn your average grocery cheesecake into something special. Arrange chocolate-dipped strawberries on top of the cheesecake.
- Dip a spoon in melted chocolate and wave it over the top of the cheesecake to make an abstract design.
- Top the cheesecake with white, dark, or milk chocolate curls or shavings. To make curls, run a vegetable peeler over room-temperature chocolate. To make chocolate shavings, use a cheese grater and grate the chocolate over the top of the cheesecake.
- A slice of a store-bought or homemade dessert can become extra special. Fill a plastic squeeze bottle with chocolate sauce or

pureed fruit sauce and write a message such as "Happy Birthday" or simply add dots and lines.

- Sprinkle confectioners' sugar on top of your dessert or all around the edge of the dessert plate for a festive touch.
- Before writing a message on your cake, place a string across the cake to make a guideline. Write just above it and then gently pull the string away when done.
- If you do not have a pastry bag for piping handy, a great substitute is a zip-type bag. Fill the bag halfway with icing, cut off the very end of the corner, and squeeze the bag.
- Decorating with melted chocolate is simple. Place chocolate chips or chocolate pieces in a zip-type bag. Place in a bowl of hot water or microwave for a short time, just until melted. Snip off the very tip of one of the corners and squeeze.

Baking Tips

- When whisking or hand mixing, wrap a damp kitchen towel around the bottom of the bowl to hold it in place.
- Keep recipe cards at eye level by placing the card in the tines of a fork. Use a water glass to hold the fork for easy reading.
- For even baking and quick cleanup, line your baking sheets with parchment paper.
- Use a small ice cream scoop to distribute

batter evenly when baking cupcakes and muffins.

- When slicing soft cookie dough, use dental floss to make clean, even cuts.
- When baking several batches of cookies, be sure to allow the baking sheet to cool off between batches so that the cookie dough does not melt.
- Do not open the door of the oven during baking. It will lower the temperature and may cause your cake to fall.
- To test baking powder, add 1/2 teaspoon of it to 1/4 cup of hot water. If it bubbles, the baking powder is still active.

11

Secrets About Food Safety

Every day the information we learn about food safety increases. You can never be too careful when it comes to food preparation and safety precautions. Pay attention to each and every item you are cooking, cleaning, and purchasing to avoid any problems. Stay up-to-date on food facts.

This chapter only scratches the surface when it comes to food safety, so get the facts from your grocer and be a smart consumer. And just in case you don't know what to do or all else fails, do what my mother always told me: "When in doubt, throw it out!"

Safety Secrets at the Grocery Store

- Shop for meat, poultry, and seafood last, and place them in plastic bags when possible to keep the packages from dripping on the other foods in your cart.
- Buy products labeled "keep refrigerated"

only if they are stored in a refrigerated case and are cold to the touch.

- Feel frozen foods to make sure they are rock solid.
- Choose canned goods that are free of dents, cracks, rust, or bulging lids.
- Never buy anything that has been tampered with or appears to be damaged. Do others a favor and report any unsafe sighting to your grocer.
- Check packages for holes, tears, and open corners. Inspect everything you purchase! Some packages even have a 1-800 consumer information number in case you have a question about their product. When in doubt, ask!

Safety Tips in the Kitchen

- Use a refrigerated thermometer to check that your refrigerator is cooling at 35° to 40° F. Your freezer should be below 0° F.
- If you have a power outage, keep your refrigerator and freezer closed. Poultry should be safe for 4 to 6 hours refrigerated and 1 to 2 days frozen. Also, frozen foods that remain cold or that have ice crystals can safely be refrozen. Discard any food that is not cold or has thawed. If in doubt, throw it out.
- Space items in your refrigerator and freezer so that air can circulate freely.
- Freeze fresh meat, poultry, and fish immediately if you don't plan to use them within a

few days. Always overwrap packages with aluminum foil or freezer wrap to make them airtight. Date them so that you know how long they've been in the freezer.

- Wrap raw meat, poultry, and fish and place them in separate plastic bags. Set them on a plate on the lowest shelf in your refrigerator to keep juices from dripping on the other foods or refrigerator surfaces.
- Follow the "use by," "keep refrigerated," and "safe handling" information on the package labels. If you cannot remember when a food was placed in the refrigerator, throw it out.
- Use refrigerated beef steaks, roasts, deli meats, and poultry within 3 to 4 days. Ground meat, ground poultry, and fish should be used within 1 to 2 days.

Pantry Storage Tips

- *Low-acid canned goods:* These are good for 2 to 5 years. This includes canned meat and poultry, stews, soups (except tomato), pastas, potatoes, corn, carrots, spinach, beans, beets, peas, and pumpkin. Check cans carefully.
- *High-acid canned goods:* These are good for 12 to 18 months. This includes tomato products, fruits, sauerkraut, dressings, and foods in vinegar-based sauces.
- Never store any foods labeled "keep refrigerated" in the pantry. Such foods must be stored in the refrigerator.

Before You Cook

- Wash your hands with hot soapy water for at least 20 seconds before starting food preparation.
- Keep everything that touches food clean. Bacteria can reside on dirty utensils, sponges, dishrags, plates, cutting boards, and hands.
- Keep raw meat, poultry, and fish and their juices from coming into contact with other foods during preparation, especially foods that won't be cooked. Wash your hands and all utensils and surfaces with hot soapy water after contact with raw meat.
- Carefully wash cutting boards with hot soapy water and then sanitize them with a solution of household bleach and water (check bleach label for directions).
- Never chop fresh vegetables or salad ingredients on a cutting board that was used for raw meat without properly cleaning it first.
- Regularly clean refrigerator surfaces with hot soapy water.
- Thaw foods only in the refrigerator or microwave oven. Never leave them out at room temperature. When you use a microwave for thawing, finish cooking immediately.
- Use a nonmetallic container when marinating meat, poultry, and seafood. Place the container in the refrigerator, not on the kitchen counter. Discard any leftover marinade that was in contact with the raw meat, or boil the

marinade for a minute before using it on cooked meat.

- Thoroughly rinse poultry and seafood in cold water and check for any strange odors before cooking.
- Wash all fresh fruits and vegetables with cold running water, using a brush to scrub them if necessary.

Cooking Thoroughly

- Cook eggs until the yolk and white are firm, not runny. Throw away or modify recipes with uncooked or partially cooked eggs.
- Do not eat raw cookie dough or taste any raw or partially cooked meat, poultry, fish, or egg dish.
- Use a meat thermometer or a quick-read thermometer to take the guesswork out of cooking meat and poultry. Place the thermometer at the thickest portion of the meat, not touching any bone or fat or the bottom of the pan.
- Roast meat and poultry in oven temperatures of 325° F. or above. Avoid prolonged low temperatures when cooking meats, which may encourage bacteria growth before cooking is complete.
- Never partially heat foods and then refrigerate or set them aside to finish cooking later. Partially cooked foods may not reach a temperature high enough to destroy bacteria.
- Cook ground beef until it is no longer pink.

- When basting grilled meats, brush sauce on cooked surfaces only. Be careful not to contaminate fully cooked meats by reusing leftover marinade or adding sauces with a brush previously used on raw meats.
- Stir, rotate, and cover foods when microwaving for even cooking. Check temperature with a quick-read thermometer in at least three spots and follow recommended standing times outside the microwave so that the food is completely cooked. Clean the interior of the microwave thoroughly after cooking.

Safe Serving

- Always place cooked food in a clean dish for serving and use clean utensils. Never use the same unwashed plate that held raw meat, poultry, or fish to serve the cooked meat.
- Do not allow any uncooked food to sit out at room temperature for more than 2 hours. When serving from a buffet, keep cold foods on ice at a temperature below 40° F. and keep hot foods above 140° F. until they are eaten. Don't mix fresh food with food that has already been out for serving.

Safe Food Away from Home

- Carry lunches in an insulated container with a freezer pack or include a frozen juice box or small plastic bottle of frozen water. Keep your lunch away from direct sunlight.

• Pack prechilled picnic food in a cooler with a freezer pack or ice. Do not use your cooler to chill room-temperature foods. When possible, use one cooler for beverages, since this is opened often, and a separate one that can be kept closed for perishable foods.

• Wrap raw meat, poultry, and fish, or place them in sealed storage bags or covered containers to avoid leakage onto other foods in the cooler (or use a separate cooler). Use moistened towelettes before and after handling the raw meat or bring a bottle filled with clean water and soap to wash hands and surfaces.

• Cut in the middle of hamburgers to make sure the meat is no longer pink before serving.

• At salad bars and buffets, check to be sure serving containers have a clean, sanitary appearance, and make sure cold foods are kept chilled and entrées are steaming hot.

Safe Leftovers

• Refrigerate cooked foods promptly after serving them (within 2 hours after cooking). You do not need to cool food first, but do divide large amounts of leftovers into smaller portions and place them in shallow containers for quick chilling.

- Freeze leftovers that you won't eat within a few days.
- Cover and reheat any leftovers to 165° F. (steaming hot). Stir foods while you reheat them to ensure that all food reaches the appropriate temperature. Reheat sauces, soups, and gravies to a rolling boil for at least one minute before serving.
- Never taste-test leftover food that looks or smells strange to judge whether you can still use it. When in doubt, throw it out!
- Dispose of potentially unsafe food in a garbage disposal or in a tightly wrapped package so it cannot be eaten by animals.

Ten Common Food-Safety Mistakes

- Countertop thawing
- Leftovers left out
- Unclean cutting board
- Room-temperature marinating
- Store-to-refrigerator lag time
- Barbecue blunder: same platter for raw and grilled meats
- Restaurant "doggie bag" delay
- Stirring and tasting spoon
- Same knife for trimming raw meat and chopping vegetables
- Hiding and eating Easter eggs

Holiday Celebrations

- Serve smaller party dishes and refill food from the refrigerator or from a hot pot on the stove.
- Do not stuff a holiday bird ahead of time, because this can encourage bacteria to grow.
- Bake stuffing separately when possible, especially with turkeys larger than 16 pounds, or confirm that the stuffing has reached 165° F. before removing the bird from the oven.
- Remove stuffing and store it separately.

12

Measurement Reference Guide

The following tips and conversion list will help you save time when cooking and preparing meals. Some cooks are natural-born chefs when it comes to seasoning or measuring food, while some of us can even ruin rice. Follow this measurement guide for accuracy, and try to stick to the amounts specified when following a recipe. While creativity counts in the kitchen, it's good to make sure you get things right, unless you have the time and excess food to experiment with!

Measurement Tips

- Measure ingredients accurately. Use glass measures for liquids. For solids or dry ingredients, use metal or plastic measuring cups and fill them to overflowing, then level them off with a knife.
- Before measuring honey or syrup, grease the measuring cup with vegetable oil and rinse it in hot water.

Conversion Tips

- a pinch or a dash = slightly less than $1/8$ tablespoon
- 1 teaspoon = 60 drops
- 3 teaspoons = 1 tablespoon
- 2 tablespoons = 1 ounce liquid
- 4 tablespoons = $1/4$ cup
- 1 cup liquid = 8 fluid ounces
- 2 cups liquid = 1 pint = $1/2$ quart
- 4 quarts liquid = 1 gallon
- 1 tablespoon butter = $1/8$ stick = $1/2$ ounce
- 2 tablespoons butter = $1/4$ stick = 1 ounce
- 4 tablespoons butter = $1/4$ cup = $1/2$ stick = 2 ounces
- 8 tablespoons butter = $1/2$ cup = 1 stick = 4 ounces
- 32 tablespoons butter = 4 sticks = 16 ounces = 1 pound
- 1 cup heavy cream = 2 cups whipped
- 1 gallon = 4 quarts = 8 pints = 16 cups = 128 fluid ounces = 3.79 liter
- $1/2$ gallon = 2 quarts = 4 pints = 8 cups = 64 fluid ounces = 1.89 liter
- $1/4$ gallon = 1 quart = 2 pints = 4 cups = 32 fluid ounces = .95 liter
- $1/2$ quart = 1 pint = 2 cups = 16 fluid ounces = .47 liter
- $1/4$ quart = $1/2$ pint = 1 cup = 8 fluid ounces = .24 liter
- 1 pound cheddar or other medium-hard cheese = 4 cups shredded

- $1/4$ pound Parmesan or other hard cheese = $1^1/4$ cups grated
- 1 pound granulated sugar = 2 cups
- 1 pound confectioners' sugar = $3^1/2$ cups sifted
- 1 pound brown sugar 5 21/4 cups firmly packed
- 1 pound white flour = 4 cups
- 1 pound whole wheat flour = $4^1/2$ cups
- 1 cup semisweet chocolate chips = 6-ounce bag
- 1 cup chocolate wafer crumbs = 19 chocolate wafers
- 1 cup vanilla wafer crumbs = 22 vanilla wafers
- 1 cup graham cracker crumbs = 14 graham cracker squares
- 1 cup uncooked long-grain rice plus 2 cups liquid = 3 cups cooked rice
- 1 cup uncooked converted rice = 4 cups cooked
- 1 cup uncooked spaghetti = 4 cups cooked
- 2 slices bread = 1 cup bread crumbs
- 1 pound cheese = 2 cups grated
- 4 ounces nuts = $3/4$ cup chopped nuts
- 1 large egg white = 2 tablespoons
- 1 large egg yolk = 1 tablespoon
- 1 medium lemon = 2 tablespoons juice
- 1 medium orange = $1/3$ cup juice
- apples, sliced raw, 1 pound = 3 cups
- carrots sliced, 1 pound = 3 cups
- onions, chopped or sliced, 1 pound = 3 cups
- 1 pound cabbage = 4 cups shredded or coarsely chopped

- 1 medium carrot = $1/2$ cup chopped or sliced
- 1 medium celery rib = $1/2$ cup chopped or sliced
- 1 cup fresh corn kernels = 2 to 3 ears
- 1 medium garlic clove = $1/2$ teaspoon finely chopped
- 1 pound mushrooms = 3 cups sliced
- 1 large sweet pepper = 1 cup coarsely chopped
- 1 medium tomato = $1/2$ cup chopped
- 1 pound potatoes = $31/2$ cups sliced or 2 cups cooked and mashed
- 1 pound romaine = 20 leaves or approximately 16 cups romaine pieces
- 1 pound iceberg lettuce = 10 cups pieces or 8 cups shredded
- 1 pound chicory = 12 cups pieces or 10 cups packed
- 1 pound fresh spinach yields approximately $11/2$ cups cooked spinach

Index

Divide and conquer your surroundings on your way to a more organized and less chaotic life with the help of . . .

ROBYN FREEDMAN SPIZMAN

GETTING ORGANIZED

This is required reading for anyone who runs a household and wants to save time, money, and energy! Organization is a monumental job for most of us, but with Robyn Freedman Spizman's systematic approach, creating a manageable environment can be a snap.

Tips for getting organized:

- Remove your name from junk-mail lists.
- Request doctor visits at times that minimize the wait—such as the first appointment of the day or right after lunch.
- No junk drawers allowed.
- And many, many more!

KITCHEN 101

Setting up a kitchen can be a daunting job for new homeowners and cooking novices. But even so-called veterans can be clueless when it comes to stocking a pantry or determining food freshness. KITCHEN 101 offers quick tips from setup to cleanup, including:

- How to prepare food basics like omelettes, pasta, and baked potatoes
- Which herbs you should always have on your spice shelf
- How to get the most out of your weekly shopping trip
- Ways to get the best use from your microwave or barbecue

MEALS IN MINUTES

MEALS IN MINUTES is a collection of simple recipes for low-fat foods that can be made quickly and easily. From appetizers to desserts, this book offers healthful alternatives to fast food.

QUICK TIPS FOR BUSY PEOPLE

Always on the run? Do you find yourself in a race against time? QUICK TIPS FOR BUSY PEOPLE is the perfect solution for anyone who is on the go and wants to save time, money, and energy.

Available next month.